MY ONLINE DATING EXPERIENCE

My Online Dating Experience

I Believe in
My Success
and Yours Too

George D. Liu

Columbus, Ohio

The views and opinions expressed in this book are solely those of the author and do not reflect the views or opinions of Gatekeeper Press. Gatekeeper Press is not to be held responsible for and expressly disclaims responsibility of the content herein.

My Online Dating Experince

Published by Gatekeeper Press
2167 Stringtown Rd, Suite 109
Columbus, OH 43123-2989
www.GatekeeperPress.com

Copyright © 2022 by George D. Liu

All rights reserved. Neither this book, nor any parts within it may be sold or reproduced in any form or by any electronic or mechanical means, including information storage and retrieval systems, without permission in writing from the author. The only exception is by a reviewer, who may quote short excerpts in a review.

Library of Congress Control Number: 2021952053

ISBN (paperback): 9781662919046
eISBN: 9781662919053

Contents

My Biography vii

Prologue 1

Chapter One: A Surprising Email 5

Chapter Two: Passionately in Love 7

Chapter Three: Love From Our Hearts 23

Chapter Four: I Have to See You First
(Heartbroken) 47

Chapter Five: Key Points of the Possible
Fraudulence 55

My Biography

George D. Liu

George D. Liu (刘道生) graduated from Wuhan Medical School in China in 1976. He did medical research at Johns Hopkins University School of Medicine in 1987. He entered into graduate school at the University of Minnesota in 1989, where he studied Biophysics. He has been a columnist for MN TIMES (明州时报) from 2016 to the present.

Publications

1. George D. Liu et al, *Genetic Metabolic Diseases* (遗传性代谢病学), 1984.

2. George D. Liu et al, *Molecular Biology for Medical Students* (医用分子生物学, 教科书), 1987.

3. George D. Liu, *Mao Zedong's School Days* (毛泽东求学记), 2021.

Prologue

ONLINE DATING IS the new way for people who are looking for someone as a friend or partner to find them. It's really wonderful, easy and enjoyable. The data shows that many people have gotten to know each other that way, and become friends, then finally a couple as husband and wife. This really means something special.

I got divorced not long ago. I am a traditional, conservative person, particularly not very good at computer science and technology (that is to say, my computer skills are not good at all). I was really reluctant to give online dating a try. However, my social activities and friend circles are very limited, so I made a decision to search for an online dating site. I found one that looked very encouraging, attractive and amazing. It said that a lot of people participate in their site, and gave statistics such as:

- 120,000+ new members register monthly
- safe & secure
- exclusive community aged 50+

Most important is that online dating provides a very good platform for a person to search for who is the best one for them, without limitations of time, location, nationality and so on.

My story of online dating is quite special. Basically, my personality is to always look at people in a positive way. I am writing a book about a great historical figure, Mr. Su (Dongpo) of the Song dynasty. Mr. Su once said, "No one people in the world is a bad guy." I totally believe that.

After I registered my profile at the online dating site, I become very popular. So many of the other registered members visited my profile, and saw some interest in me. That's not all. Only a few days after I registered, I got a special email from a lady who was a member of the same site. She was a very positive person as well, and she found the best guy she was looking for. She was very enthusiastic to introduce a lady she knew well to me. She said, "I believe if my story can be successful, yours will be too. Good luck!!!"

I believed her and trusted her. From that point, an unbelievable love story began, of a type I had never had before.

This love story is not very long, so please read, and send your thoughts to me. My email address is: george.liu31@gmail.com.

Good luck!!!

I hope your experiences at online dating will be great and successful!!!

George D. Liu
July 17, 2021

Love doesn't have to be so complicated. You can do it.

I believe if my story can be successful, yours can be too.

Good luck!!!

CHAPTER ONE
A Surprising Email

Thursday, June 24, 2021

Sue wrote an email to me (3G).

Hi 3G:

I'm writing to inform you that my story has been a success on this site as I found my life partner and we are getting married soon.

I was online today, about closing my account when my friend Fantasy (who has been so reluctant giving the online dating a try) came across your profile. She's been all over me about getting in touch with you . . . Lol.

Anyway she's 61 years old, 5'11 Tall, Widower, a good Listener, Beautify Lady. I really do not know if you have found someone already, but I thought I take a chance, you never know until you try, it might worth it at the end of the day. Please take a chance and email her, she'll share a picture and more information with you, her direct email is: XXXX@gmail.com.

One thing I can assure you is you'll brighten her day if you do get in touch with her.

Am closing my account now with this little hint, and I believe if my story can be successful, yours will be too. Good luck!!!

Sue

CHAPTER TWO
Passionately in Love

I followed the suggestion from the surprising email. An unbelievable love story began.

Thursday, June 24, 2021

I wrote an email to Fantasy.

Hi Fantasy:

Your friend, Sue, introduce you to me. It's very nice of her. I just opened my account in this online dating site. Please introduce yourself to me with basic information. My cell phone number is XXX-XXX-XXXX. Please text me first before you call because I don't answer the phone which I don't know. I am a writer, honest, intelligent . . . , and easy person also. I am waiting for your email. Let us start from somewhere there.

By your friend I think you are a good girl. I always

treat people with respect. I don't like people fight each other at all. Hopefully you understand what I mean.

Thank you for your time to read my email. 3G

Friday, June 25, 2021

Fantasy wrote an email back.

Hello 3G:

How are you doing? My friend told me you will contact me, and am really happy to hear from you because l never knew you will get back to me but you did.

Here's little more about me:

I'm Fantasy Mullberry 61 years old, 5'11 Tall and I am Originally from Milan Italy and I grew up in Holand but l live in Mahatun, New York. before we can move on, l hope long distance is not a problem for you? My Friend And Her Husband Just Met on XYXY Dating Site, am really happy about this, so that what makes me to tell her to send you note, maybe l can be lucky to have my other half l have been missing very long time too LOL! Well am ready to relocate and move on with my dream man if anything works fine in between me and him.

I'm blessed with a grandmother in Holand l got degree in Marketing so am into selling and buying of Sports Culture for some large multinational corporations, Museums and Malls, and l have been doing that for about 30 years now, l will tell you more about this in my next email.

I enjoy reading, boating, hiking, traveling, swimming, fishing, nature, walks on the beach, watching sunsets, movies, listening music, and quiet nights at home... I am a God fearing woman and i was raised with a very strict catholic background with good morals and values, i am honest, I do not cheat or play games or drama, I can't stand seeing someone been intentionally hurt, fight and struggle each other. I have had my heart broken before, and I will never pass that kind of pain to a man. I'm a simple woman with a big heart you will find that l am very caring, understanding, patient, loving and kind.

I am full of passion and romance, and have an endless amount of love to offer the right man. I'm searching to find that one man that will take my breath away, the one man that I can never stop thinking of for any reason, the one man that the mere whisper of his name brings a smile to my face. He must be not only my best friend, but also my soul mate so tell me more about you too.

Kindly see the attachment,

My **pictures** are attached to this email so have a fabulous day today!

Regards,
Fantasy.

Attached photos:

Friday, June 25, 2021

I wrote back to Fantasy.

Dear Fantasy:

You are very nice lady as your friend Sue said. Love should come from heart as you did. I came USA in March 1987 and I am lucky I can stay in the country I like. Every people had something before. I think love can drive bad lucky we had out of our life.

From now on we should focus on our future. I did have some past unhappy time. Finally it is over now. I can tell you what stories I had in the past. My cellphone # is XXX-XXX-XXXX. You can call me anytime it's better text me first before you call because I generally don't answer that call I don't know. I hope you understand what I am saying.

I only have one daughter, she is wonderful, married, working for the big health company in US. However, she doesn't want kids. It means I don't have any grandchildren.

I graduated from medical school in CCC. I am very healthy, do not take any medication. I believe we can do a lot of things if we come together. The book of preliminary version that talks about trading stock is done, English version needs to be finalized. CCC version can be finalized anytime. You know several languages, we can finalize the English version together. Of course, everything depends on what your thoughts.

I hope we can come together for our future life.

Sincerely yours, 3G

Saturday, June 26, 2021

Fantasy wrote back to me.

Hello 3G:

    Thank you for your response and taking me on a little journey in your world, and I appreciate your patience and zeal in telling me things about you, with the main aim of me getting to know you better as an open book. I have a son (25), he is actually Gay (homosexual) and he is married to a 40 years old man :). He lives in Manchester and runs a Restaurant with his partner. Initially we had a very distant relationship when I first discovered he was not straight. It was hard to take in because he was my only son, and I wanted grandchildren. Anyway that is a long time ago and now I have accepted him for who he is, and I try to appreciate him that way. Our relationship is a very complex one with ups and downs, but I try to remember that life is short and enjoy it all the same. Sometimes I tend to feel guilty about not showing him enough love as a child, because I wanted to toughen him up and maybe this had the wrong effect on his sexuality by seeking fatherly love elsewhere. I don't know why I still believe his sexual orientation is a Phenotypic factor and not a Genetic one.

    As a result of growing up in different cultures, I can eat almost anything, I'm very adventurous towards food. I'm sure at this point you can tell I am always very direct and straight forward. I'm inclined to be very spontaneous, I tell you precisely what is on my mind when I feel it and this has made me a honest person naturally. I don't usually use age as a very important factor when I'm seeking a true companion. I'm looking for a true companion and a permanent partner. However, I feel if you are going to find that person you have to take things slowly and start out as friends and let things proceed from there.

I discovered going to Karaoke a few years ago and I think it is a very nice way to have fun and enjoy yourself. I like to sing but my voice limits my singing to a very basso kind :). I used to smoke but I quit in 2004. I still drink occasionally but it is usually Champagne or Red Wine. I'm also a very Optimistic and Open Minded person. Being Optimistic and Open minded has always attracted others to me. Although internet dating is new to me, I do think you are a sincere and Honest person.

I just felt like sending you a message on the topics of conversation we would be having if I was in the same room with you. So now its your turn. Let me know something about yourself that you would usually not tell people when you first meet them. Or maybe you can just tell me what you were like when you were younger.

PS: I certainly can't wait for this virus to be over already so that life can go back to normal.

Take care
Fantasy.

Saturday, June 26, 2021

I wrote back to Fantasy.

Dear Fantasy:
You are very nice and kind. I totally understand your feelings what you had in mind.

This is first time for me getting into internet dating starting from June 17, 2021. You might not believe that I just officially got divorce on June 15th. Actually my wife and I separated in early 2017, It means no sexual relationship. I bought a mobile home in April 2019. The house my wife and I lived was paid off, value of that house around $XXX,XXX if selling now. Unfortunately, my wife's right foot got fracture on September 23, 2019. I went back to take care of her until she could walk. Cutting long story to short, actually she always says divorce, but never does it. I was patient, I was always there whenever she needed me. Therefore I think I am a good people and responsible person. My daughter understands the relationship between her mother and me. As you know Covid-19, my divorce was done through Court Hearing with Zoom meeting by my daughter help at my daughter house. I am proud of my daughter who is smart, and what she has done and can do for me. That is my story. I should say, my wife is a good person, nothing wrong with her, she worked hard, never missed any workday. Whatever I did for her and her family I think I should be because I was her husband. As a husband I was responsible for whenever she needed me.

Now I am not her husband, I have right to look for my best partner to move forward. People's life is short, every one has right to find their soulmate to get a better life in the future as soon as possible.

Now you know what my past was. You should feel free saying "No" to me if you think I am not right man for you. I sincerely hope you are happy.

I am looking forward to hearing your decision from you!

Sincerely yours, 3G

Saturday, June 26, 2021

Fantasy wrote back to me.

Hello 3G:

Always nice to read from you as well! One thing of a certainty is that first impression matters a lot, the chemistry and connection from the first conversation can help to be a good determinant of where things could possibly lead to and I am feeling positive so far as we seem to have a vibe that goes along with each other. I am glad that you are in line with my opinion on how to build a solid foundation for an ever lasting relationship.

Over the years, I have learned and come to realize that life comes in its seasons, I have had my fair share of being hurt and heart broken and I have also had times when I was living my best life feeling on top of the world with no problems. So right now I am carrying along the positive and leaving behind all the bad experience only keeping the lessons from them, and I have decided that from now henceforth, i only choose happiness and that is what I am chasing. From when I was little, I have read books where the couple ended up happily ever after but I have never experienced that . . . if that is what you are chasing and willing to experience at this stage of your life, then I believe that we are on the same path.

I like a person that is trustworthy and stays straightforward with me irrespective of the situation, and I hate disloyalty and not being able to put my all where I have my heart cause the other party don't really got you like that so like every other lady, I like to be rest assured that no one else can take my place! I have no tattoos and just the regular ear piercings. I love r&b, blues and some nice hip hop music whenever I want to dance and let loose, do you like dancing?! I enjoy seafood and I prefer homemade cooking to eating out, simply because I know I could always do better at cooking nice better meals than even the restaurant, a lady gotta be proud of her skills right?! LOL!

After reading your last message, I have chosen to tell you some important aspects about my life from the beginning. My parents met in Holand and the connection and chemistry according to them was out of this world. After they got married, they had only one daughter (me) and decided to keep it that way. We stayed in Holand for about 11 years where my dad tried to pursue a career as a Professional Antiques Art collector. I got my passion for art from my dad but later he decided we would be happier in the UK when he got an opening to become a professor of Archaeology. So that's how I ended up spending most of my teen years in London. I met my late husband while I was at the Art Institute of Chicago. He was a very smart, Handsome man, we were very good friends and after graduating from the University, we did not see each other for about 4 years. The next time we had the opportunity to meet again we decided we wanted to be together forever. He passed away in December 2012 after a long battle with the leukemia.

My mother is 82 years old, lives in nursing home with a small circle of friends, and the fasility keeps them active and busy. She's fairly healthy for her age and that makes me happy. I reach out to her about twice a week, and when I'm in Manchester I always try to visit her as often as I can, even though I feel it's not enough.

One thing I never do is regret and it is because my mind has brought me to the level of understanding of the Human world that I have today. Since I have been widowed, I did not try dating until in 2015. I was in a brief relationship that nothing really ever came out of. I believe that every phase of the life has its own purpose. Yes, I do not exist in the past because I have always believed what I am LIVING in the HERE AND NOW!! TODAY is a gift that is why it is called the PRESENT!

Asides travelling all over the world selling and buying sports Culture, I'm a fine artist, I do work on several types of paintings and I organize showrooms

My Online Dating Experience 17

and auctions for sports art and goods sales. My love for sports art initially didn't help me with my travelling around the world making sales, I was actually only painting buying and selling as a side hustle while I was travelling about executing work related projects for a company I worked with which was primarily involved in the developing and processing of SEMICONDUCTOR materials in the High purity sector. I enjoy what I do because art is life!

I have incessantly desired to explore the American landscape and the move to New York has been very fulfilling in many different ways for me. I am unable to really say I'm living the dream, however I think happiness is basically something we give ourselves. I travel a great deal for work and pleasure but I'm about to eliminate travelling for work altogether. Exploring the globe is a hobby I hope to continuously undertake for the rest of my days on this planet. I was born into a Christian home but as time passed, the circumstances surrounding me made it imperative that I experienced other ways of life while growing up.

I'm inquisitive about many things including: history, humanity and world cultures. I enjoy modelling for hobby, taking beautiful pictures by the beach or just generally. Nature has a therapeutic and positive effect upon my spirit, in addition to its beauty, it makes me feel connected to the Universe. That doesn't mean I don't enjoy the pleasure of just relaxing at home. I have come to acknowledge the fact that I am a practical individual who is complex some times but established in a few values that I believe are universally good. Am I perfect? Certainly not! Who is? But my sincere desire is always to understand and make use of my imperfections, with the intention to become the best that I could possibly be as an ordinary functioning woman.

Do you still have a profile on XYXY Dating site?! I must confess I already find you very interesting and I can hardly wait to read a message from you.

Regards,
Fantasy.

Saturday, June 26, 2021

I wrote back to Fantasy.

Dear Fantasy:

You are so nice to me. Every person's family is unique in the world. You had your parents story. My one even worse.

My mother came to my home as child bride because her mom was my dad's mom's sister. Unfortunately, my mom just got pregnant (me), my dad was died on fire in the workplace before I was born. He died in August 1949, I was born in December 1949. When I was born, having 4 people in my family were my grandma, my mom, my aunt (my dad's sister) and me. Whole family life was miserable. In that time no labour worker in my family meant no hope in the countryside. My mom had to get married again. After my mom got re-married, gave birth of another 7 children. 5 of them have been survived. It means that my family is a complex family.

Because of complex situation I always did my best to get jobs done well. You know special environment could make me independent from when I was a young boy.

I think I did very well. I have very good reputation in my home countryside. I have made an example for young generation there. Actually I did achieve a lot of things.

I am not wealthy, but no problem to maintain basic life. In the meantime, there are some potentials for me to do. You are good at marketing, which is important for you and me, of course, if you and I can come together. I have written book that talking about how to trade stock in market, it's important for people to know and trade stock. If you and I can come together, we can speed up publishing process, the key is how to convince people to buy. My book is unique, no people write as I do.

Something else we can do as well . . .

When I registered dating in the internet, many people seem to have interested in, try to pursue who they like. You know world is big, I only need one who really loves me, cares each other. In my opinion health is most important part. Sometimes health even more important than money. I don't know what your thoughts are.

I like you. However, I can not be so selfish. I let you make your mind who you really like. This is a big difficult decision, you have to think over. You talk about sexual, and chemistry, when decision is made, chemistry should not be problem at all. For me I can do anything for Who I Like. I not only hope you love me, but also I will do everything possible to keep you in good health as long as I can do. My mom is alive, 94 years old now. I hope you and I can live as long as over 100 years old . . . .

I'm short than you. Do you mind? Of course, I like my soulmate the more beautiful the better.

I am looking forward to hearing your final decision from you.

Sincerely yours, 3G

Monday June 28, 2021

I wrote again to Fantasy.

Dear Fantasy:
You are my angel. You know you are in my heart, I probably have everything you hope except for wealthy because I just got divorced, I gave everything to my ex wife in order to warranty she can have a good life.

You have much more talent, my ex wife even could not understand English well. If You and I come together we can do much more, working together make tomorrow brighter.

I tell you my case, the purpose is to let you know our future depends on you and me. I have to do this, I don't want to lie to you. In doing so I tell you my story the earlier the better. Otherwise, you may complain what I didn't tell you earlier. Please understand me.

You're not only beautiful, but also understand me. You make me happy. Every word you wrote to me is meaningful. You spiritually encourage me, you make me smile, heart beat up . . . . . . , of course sex desire as well. This is not every girl who can do except for you, I like you, and also I want you happy, I don't want to cheat you, and let you know who I am.

Please forgive me if I did something wrong. The stock book I am writing is good for any stock traders to know. I'm sure your English much better than mine. If you and I do good job on it, it might make some fortunes. Of course, we can do something else also.

I wrote to you to express what my feelings are. If what I do here bother you, please forgive me.

Sincerely yours, 3G

Fantasy wrote back to me.

Hello 3G,
You can text me on my number XXX XXX XXXX so that we can communicate more better.

Dear Fantasy:
OK. What time is good for us to talk? Where are you now? 3G

Dear Fantasy:
My phone does not allow me to add your phone number, it said it is not valid #. Please text me at XXX-XXX-XXXX, and call me anytime. 3G

Dear Fantasy:

The phone# you gave is wrong #, no answer. Please call me at XXX-XXX-XXXX, before 5:30 or after 6:30pm, because 5:30→ 6:30pm, I'm going to swim.

Thank you for your consideration. 3G

CHAPTER THREE
Love From Our Hearts

The texting messages' conversations start in the afternoon, **Monday, June 28, 2021**.

>Fantasy: Hello!
>Please who is this?
>**3G: I wonder who you are?**
>F: Alright Why do you ask that?
>**3G: Fantasy.**
>F: Yes, Am Fantasy.
>**3G: May call you? Or you call me.**
>(No phone call occurred at all . . . . . .)

Tuesday, June 29, 2021

I wrote an email to Fantasy.

Dear Fantasy:
 You're my angel. I hope you always happy. Please do me a favor, use the email for our communication. What

you need to do is do your best to write what your mind tells you. You and I have to do this, please understand me. Please let me know if you agree. I am yours. Please trust me.

Actually we had good email communications for last few days. Just continue to do it.

Sincerely yours, 3G

F: Hello good morning!

How was your night?

3G: Very Good. Thank you.

F: what are you doing.

3G: I miss you, in the same time I am working on my writing.

How about you?

F: Are you still on XYXY Dating site.

3G: Hi Fantasy: I am not sure what you'd like to do. In my mind you are talent person, have good English skills. I said I love you. I hope you're happy. Everything is on your hands. Now I want you to use Email for our communication. I won't tell you why now. I'll tell you one month later. Can you do it?

Wednesday, June 30, 2021

3G: Dear Fantasy: Good morning! Enjoy, I try to make money from now on.

F: Are you still on XYXY Dating?

3G: Hi Fantasy: Yes. Everything is not sure yet. You did not give me anything what you concern. I wrote an email to you yesterday, you just keep silent.

I know you are very smart, can do much better than I do. Now I try to make some money from stock trade. And it is a good time to do so now. Of course, just guess. We will see in about 2 weeks. I have some idea, that's why I want you to work together with me, and get some good things done. If you agree I will write an email to you, you just put your thoughts on, send it back to me. Don't do too long, roughly one month. Would you do it?

F: Am asked you something simply and you didn't answer me.

i want you to cancel you XYXY Dating.

before we can go on and I will be dedicated to you.

3G: Are you sure you will love me and we can come together? As I told you I just got divorced, not wealthy guy, of course, I will try to make money, You understand me?

F: I understand you and am ready to go to anywhere with you if you do what i asked you.

3G: OK. Thank you. In this case, I will do what you like. First of all we should come together to work on the book talking about stock I have been writing, and speed up publishing process. I don't have any problems for you and me to live together economically. Do you agree to come my city, and live together? Do you want to see me some time soon? As I said you are my angel. I am willing to do anything if you need. You agree.

I can cancel my list in XYXY Dating today if you agree to come to my city, we live together, and work on my book together . . . .

Please tell me, you come or not?

I will wait for your answer, and take action then.

I really love you, and live together for the rest of our life. I want you happy for our living time.

I think you understand what my thoughts are now. I will do what you want me to do. I will cancel my list on XYXY Dating today. Sincerely yours, 3G

Fantasy, you are my angel. I did what you wanted me to cancel my list in XYXY Dating.

It's cancelled already.

I hope you happy. We can come together soon. Please let me know if anything else you need me to prepare for.

F: Can you show me the proof that you have canceled it?

3G: Yes. That website has some info. Please see your email. Proof is there. You are my angel. I love you, I want to see you soon.

F: But you can still delete it not to see the account anymore.

3G: I can not get into website, my account was closed.

F: Alright I will believe you for that.

Can you send me your pictures

3G: OK. Please see email. I sent some to you already.

My Online Dating Experience

Did you see my photos yet?
Please tell me your plan for our future.
My angel: I am going to swim, back at 6:30 pm. See you later.

Friday, July 2, 2021

3G: Hi My angel: How is your day going?

Saturday, July 3, 2021

3G: Good morning! My angel. Please see your email I just wrote to you.

F: Hello 3G, how are you. I have a contract I'm working for about 3 weeks now but I'll be going to Canada for the presentation in some few days, I'll be using Private Jet and the contract is a life changing for me Because it's about $9 Millions→$18 Millions I'll be getting if I am finally awarded the contract, and at this point I'm 80% sure I'll get the contract cos I have been doing this for the past 30 years and they're considering working with someone with very long time experience so I'm the only one with that requirements. This means a lot to me and I'm putting all my best in this so it can work out well and I'm sure by God's grace I'll win the contract.

3G: Dear Fantasy: Congratulation. I am very glad to hear it. I hope you are the best, and also win it. How soon you can know the final result. What you want me to do? Please let me know.

When will you be back in the US?

Sunday, July 4, 2021

3G: Good morning! Fantasy, My angel: I support you whatever you do. I think the best way you do now is to focus on your presentation in near future, and get the contract. I hope you win and happy.

Sincerely yours, 3G

Tuesday, July 6, 2021

F: Hello!
How are you?

3G: Thank you Fantasy, my angel. I'm Very good. I am looking forward to hearing good news from you. I really hope you get the contract.

I am searching data to prepare writing a book about dealing with Rhinitis.

Please take a good care of yourself.

Sincerely yours, 3G

F: That's nice I feel.

Am just with you right now.

What are you doing now?

3G: Thank you. watch stock market, review my article for newspaper.

F: Did you invest on stock market?

3G: Yes,

F: What is the value on your stock now?

3G: It's not good now. About $XXXXX.

Now market is going down.

Do you trade stock?

F: I invest on Bitcoins.

3G: It looks like too much risks as well.

F: I know can you check through the website you might want to invest.

3G: Yes.

My problem is that I suggest trading role I didn't follow, that is why I lost some money.

Hopefully I can do a better job later.

It's easy to make money when market is stable or up.

F: Yeah I agree with that.

3G: Good!

F: What are you doing now?

3G: I took a nap. Sorry I just woke up.

Are you there?

F: Am here.

I will be traveling to Canada on Friday.

3G: When will you give your presentation?

F: By Monday sweetheart.

Have you took your dinner?

3G: Not yet.

F: Why want are you having for dinner?

3G: What do you mean?

My angel: I didn't get "why want are you having for dinner".

It's wonderful that your presentation comes soon. That is your big hope, I'll cross fingers for you.

OK, My angel, let me guess, you ask me what I will have for dinner? Actually what I really want is that you and I can come together to make a good and healthy food for our dinner.

Wednesday, July 7, 2021

F: Good morning, honey! Hope your day goes well and your night with me even better!

3G: Fantasy, Good morning, my angel, I love you and miss you. Yes, my night with you should be much better. Hope every day is good day for you.

My angel, my one old picture taken in 1985 and other are sent to you. Please see your email.

Thursday July 8, 2021

F: Hello!

3G: Hi my angel, I just came in home after I cut grass. How are you?

OK, I am going to swim. I'll be back at 4:40pm. See you later.

Hi my angel, I am back. Are you there?

Hello! My angel, Are you there?

Friday, July 9, 2021

3G: Hi Fantasy, Today is a big day for you, maybe your new turning point, please take a good sleep, have a good trip, and an excellent presentation. I'm looking forward to hearing from you.

F: Hello sweetheart.

How are you doing?

I just got to Canada.

And am so tired I wish you're here now with me

Attached photo:

Hope you love the picture.

Saturday, July 10, 2021

3G: You are wonderful girl, you know I love you. You know I go to bed early every day. I just woke up, I wish I could see your message and photo earlier. Now the most important is that take a good sleep, restore your energy.

I am so happy you get this opportunity, I am confident you can do a good job and get the contract. I am cross finger for you. I am with you my girl now. Best wishes. Sincerely yours. 3G.

My Online Dating Experience 33

F: Good morning my love.
how are you doing?
3G: Very good. Did you have a good sleep?
F: Yes, but have been down and worried.
3G: My angel: everything should be fine. Just relax a little bit. I'm very confident you can do a good job.

You can do very well. Only thing you can do now is your encouragement.

Will you have some other activities?

F: I'm broken right now my love, I AM SAD. I got a call not quite long from the TAX Clearance office that I need to pay policy and taxes fee, and am not really happy with what's happening here. I was thinking I should be paying less than $XXXX USD for the goods I purchased from CCC since what I purchased is about $1,800,000 (1.8 millions) USD and that is how it is in other parts of the world. To my greatest surprise, I was given a document to make a payment of $XX,XXX USD, this was really strange to me because I never had a plan of paying such amount of money on tax, and I have used almost all my money in purchasing my goods because it is really cheaper where I bought it just because am very sure I will make a lot of profit on them once the contract is done I am getting $18,000,000 (18 millions) USD. And I would have just use my bank card or credit card but they locked and the fraud department won't allow me to use it because I forgot to place a travel notice before I traveling down here, so I won't have access to them unless I come in person to rectify the lock and my other account is also going through upgrading process right now.

3G: I understand what you talk about. In my understanding it happened already. Worry is not useful. For the time being, just put all of these things away for a little while, focus on what you should do on your presentation. Other things you should wait until you finish your presentation. Tax issue you can deal with it after you come back. You and I can go in and solve it.

My angel, don't worry about anything else, just focus on your presentation.

From now on, don't do anything business with CCC, too much cheat there.

I wait for you to come back, you and I deal with that issues together. I really hope you can get that contract you pursued.

When will you come back?

My angel: don't tell your story to any people. Do a good job on your presentation, come back safely. I wait for you. I will do my best to deal with the issue you have.

If I sell my stock next Monday I can probably get $XX,XXX. You can use it if you need.

F: Really thanks I promise I will refund it back my love.

3G: Don't worry. You are my angel, my girl, my money is yours. I love you, I love you whatever you are.

F: You're the best and I promise I would never hurt you.

3G: I love you my girl, do your best on your presentation and get back safely. I want see you soon. I want see my beautiful girl always happy.

F: My love I want to see you soon too.

3G: You and I come together we can make money together. American has a song called "Don't worry Be happy!" I hope you are always a happy girl.

We are over 60, I know who I should love, what to do is right. I love you really from my heart.

F: Hope you're going to propose to me when you get to see me.

3G: Yes, you are my girl. I want to live with you for my life time. I hope you too.

Of course, I want to make you happy.

F: Really I'm ready to relocate for me to be with you when am back from my presentation my love.

3G: Wonderful, please let me know what else I can do for you. I have a place to live, swimming pool is close. After problem is gone we can find the best place to live.

F: Do you live with anybody or I can live in your apartment when I come over?

3G: No, only me. Very quiet place. I think you will love it. We can move if we make some money.

F: Alright when am done with the contract and the payment is ready we are going to invest and buy bigger house my love.

3G: Great. I think we can make our future brighter. I love you, I want my angel happy.

F: Hope you won't hurt my feelings my love.

3G: I will never hurt you. You are my girl. I will do my best to love you, and care of you. You will know when you see me.

F: I believe you my love.

3G: Great. I am very healthy, and energetic. When people are aging, many people's health is going down. I am not there yet. We can have much better living quality to enjoy.

F: I love your positivity mind and I appreciate how you cherish someone like me.

3G: I think you know, every people love some one, when they talk with each other, no sense at all. If I love someone I will do everything to love her like you. It means, love is power. Do you agree?

F: I agree my love.

3G: Good.

F: What are you doing now?

3G: Read CCC history story.

So many people very smart, give very intelligent thinking. I always learn from other people.

I almost finish a booklet about a plant to help patient with Rhinitis. When I see you I will tell you how wonderful the plant is.

My angel I am going to swim now.

Back at 6:30pm.

See you later.

I'm back now.

I just eat dinner. How about you.

F: My love am on bed right now I want to sleep now I will text you when I wake up.

I love you.

Have a good night sleep love you to the moon.

3G: My angel, I just woke up. I am so excited that you sleep love me to the moon. I hope you happy and sleep with me together now. Love make you and me the happiest people now. Talk to you soon, my girl.

F: It is magical to fall asleep in your arms, but it is even better to wake up next to you good morning honey.

3G: Great. It means you and I will have very good future. Thanks God send you to me. God bless you and me. I hope you have a great day today. My angel, I will love you whenever you like to be.

F: Thanks for having me in your heart and I will always appreciate it and cherish it, but am still frustrated about this because I need to pay for the tax clearance soon this week.

3G: It's fine. You tell me when you need money, I will sell my stock for paying what you need.

My girl I will always be with you. You are my girl, you should trust me. I love you, you know it.

Please figure out what account number in IRS(?) you should put money in. I can direct deposit it in if necessary.

You are my girl, I may pay it something by my credit card if you want. I think my stock money plus credit card, should have enough money to cover what you need.

I want you to take easy. Everything will be fine. Just do your best to do a good job on your presentation.

My girl: do you agree?

How much total of money you need to pay?

Are you there?

Talk to me now my girl.

I called the banker about my account in stock, I can get money afternoon of Wednesday after 4:00pm or early morning Thursday if I sell my stock Monday. What you worry about. Rest of them I can pay it by credit card.

Please let me know what you plan to do.

F: My love the money is $XX,XXX and I will get the available account ready when the money is ready at your bank what do you think my love and I really appreciate everything you have done you're the best 3G.

3G: No problem at all. I have a great trust, I don't owe any money to any people and company. You should get your account # before Wednesday. I think my credit line is about $XXXX. I can pay that a little early. Do you want me to pay all of $XX,XXX, or not.

Bank told me money should be ready on Wednesday.

F: Alright I would get the account before Wednesday.

3G: Great. You are really my good girl.

F: What is the name of your bank honey?

I promise I will refund it back as soon I got my goods.

3G: Wait for second.

F: What's that honey?

3G: For second.

F: Alright honey.

3G: I'm on the phone with credit card company. You need get phone number from the bank your account is. Then I call that bank to pay some money by credit card.

You need your account info from that bank for me to transfer money to.

I hope you understand the process that sometimes is very complicated, I have to be very careful.

My bank is XXX.

My girl you got it.

F: Alright I will get it for on Monday.

It's a wire transfer you're sending or a bank to bank transfer.

3G: I wonder account number is yours or the bank account in tax clearance

F: The account will be the tax clearance operative account from the secretary they said when am ready to make payment I should request for the account number.

3G: Money in Credit card I have to call and pay it.

My bank can transfer (?), May wire. I have to talk to my banker.

F: How much is in your credit card?

3G: Sounds great. Everything should be done on Thursday.

My credit line is $XXXX.

This is one of my credit cards.

F: Alright before Wednesday I would get the account info ready honey.

Honey hope am not inconveniencing you with your funds because I know you will need some money too.

3G: You should plan what we have to do together. We can solve any unpredictable questions when moving money.

My girl we have to solve your issue first. In doing so your bank account can be unlocked. After that both of us should be happy. Right?

You understand what I am saying.

I am quite sure your issue will be solved. You should be happy now.

F: I understand and I want to be the woman in your life forever and I promise I will never hurt your feelings and we are going to achieve our goals together.

3G: I am intelligent, we can come together and do a lot of things. Our future should be much better. I love you as I told you.

Everything I do is because you are wonderful and honest girl. You should feel how much I love you.

F: I feel so and I will forever be grateful and I love you to the moon.

3G: Thank you very much. I will never hurt you. I want to keep you happy with me.

F: I will make sure I make you happy everyday until forever.

3G: Me too. You are my wonderful girl. I have to make you happy for my life

F: Thanks so tell me what are you doing now?

3G: Cook for lunch.

F: What did you cook for lunch?

3G: Chicken with a lot of other stuff and rice.

My angel, everything should be fine. I want to see my girl with beautiful smile a great girl. I love you, I need you my good girl, I want you with me all the time together asap.

F: As soon I get this done I will be back to the state my love and I can't wait to cook a good meal for you.

3G: We do together enjoy together, I want you and me to stay together.

You know I really love you. Now I hope you take easy, do a great job on your presentation, get the contract done as you prepared for.

I really hope you and I can do a wonderful job, make our future great.

I'm going to swim. Back at 6:30pm

F: I will stay with you forever.

3G: Thank you very much. Take a good sleep. Tomorrow is a big day for you.

F: Alright baby and please dream about me and remember I love you

3G: I love you, my angel. I am sure I will dream you.

Monday, July 12, 2021

F: Hello good morning sweetheart.

3G: Good morning my angel. Don't worry anything, get your presentation done well. I will do everything you need. I am going to Home depot. Talk to you soon. 3G

Hello my angel, I am back.

F: My love am done with my presentation, it went well. I want to say a very big thanks to you baby for your encouragement, love and care, because without you I will be frustrated and down. I got the contract approved by the committee, you're the best in the world for me.

What happened at the Home Depot?

3G: My Angel: I said you are my best wonderful girl. I am very confident you can do a great job. Congratulations. I love you at all time and any time. I am looking forward to seeing you and celebrate our future to come.

F: I can't wait to see you so we can't celebrate in grand style.

3G: Yesterday the big storm damaged my stove. I am trying to fix.

F: Alright hope you're doing well.

I wish am there with you now my love.

3G: Me too. I want see my great beautiful girl my angel right now.

F: I just need to make the payment of the goods before I come back home.

3G: I am doing well. I just want to see you and stay together.

I have No any problem pay the tax clearance.

I will do very good job for it. I love you, we can solve any problems.

Will you stay in Canada for some more days?

F: As soon I get the money paid successfully I will be coming back to the state.

My Online Dating Experience

And I will like to schedule my flight to the nearest airport around you.

3G: No any problems, I prepare enough money already.

F: Have you withdrawn (sold) your stock today?

3G: Come to my city. I pick you up.

Today is a good day, stock going up now, it guarantee our money.

I can probably get $XX,XXX from stock.

That is for you and me.

Do you need money to book airline ticket?

My angel, I sold all of my stock. For sure $XX,XXX. Maybe a little more.

I have to call in, make sure how much I can use.

Yes, $XX,XXX I can use from stock. Credit card can pay another $XXXX. It means everything is covered to pay your tax as required.

My angel, are you there?

I talked to the banker for my account from stock. You should take easy now. We can pay your tax clearance as required.

My money is available Wednesday.

You and I do payment on Thursday. Ok?

F: Thanks so much I really appreciate and I promise you I will never hurt you in anyway.

You're the best.

3G: You are my girl. I'll do whatever you need. I love you. When you and I meet together, I will tell you how wonderful you are in my mind.

F: You're the best man in the world for me.

3G: You are the best girl I never meet.

I will use my heart to love you.

F: I will use my heart to be with you forever and for real.

3G: Me too. You should be confident I really love you.

F: I promise to be yours forever my love.

3G: Thank you for your big heart. I just want to see you asap.

You are the most successful girl by yourself in the world. That's why I love you. You are my glory.

In the other words I am really proud of you.

I am yours also.

F: My love I will always make you proud.

3G: You are my girl, thank you very much.

The love story You and I made is unbelievable, it's very good topic to write.

F: Am sure you would write good things about it.

3G: Of course, may take a while.

My angel: You did a wonderful job on your presentation, got the contract you want. The only thing you need to do now is to relax, enjoy, until Thursday you and I deal with the payment to tax clearance.

After that we come together enjoy together then move forward.

Thank you!

F: As soon we made the payment I will (be) come to see you.

3G: I appreciate what you have done. My beautiful

girl, this is historical change for you and me in our life time.

F: I will love you until infinity my love.

3G: My girl, I miss you, I want you with me now. I want you healthy, beautiful, always happy girl.

My angel: now I prepare to cook rice porridge with many different stuffs together for tomorrow, cook over night, it's good for health. When you come over we can enjoy together.

F: Alright I can't wait to taste your good meal.

3G: My girl, now most important is keeping our physical and spiritual health. This is special for senior people to improve their life quality.

F: Yes love you're right and I would be happy to do that together with you.

3G: Very good, I'll be very happy to do with you, enjoy our new life.

F: Am very happy too my love.

I thanks God for bringing you my way.

You're God sent and I will always cherish you my love.

3G: Me too. I never expect to find one like you for my life. You are so great, you did everything yourself for many years, and so successfully done, got whatever you want. This is not every person can do it except for you. I love you and respect you.

You are really my angel, I hope both of us happy, live together over 100 years old.

F: I pray so and I promise never to hurt your feelings.

CHAPTER FOUR

I Have to See You First (Heartbroken)

Tuesday, July 13, 2021

3G: Hi My angel, good morning. Could you call me at XXX-XXX-XXXX, we can discuss how to pay the Tax clearance asap before we do it Thursday.

F: My love are you there.
Good morning!

3G: Very good. How about you?

F: Am good and I wish you're here.

3G: Thank you. Can you call me at XXX-XXX-XXXX.

F: I would be (I went) out to get some documents, I will call you when am back.

3G: Ok!

F: What are you doing now?

3G: Exercise.

F: My love.

3G: I am back.

F: Are you still busy.

3G: OK now. You can call me.

F: Alright I miss you and I wish you're here with me.

3G: Call me now.

Why don't you call me now.

F: My love 😍 it's so nice hearing your sweet voice I love it 🥰

I can't wait for we to be together so that we can share good memories together.

3G: I have to see my angel before paying. My money is ready, just want to see you first.

F: My love 😍 I will come over when am done with the payment here.

Why do you doubt the love and affection I got for you.

Do you think I'll run away with your money.

3G: I didn't say that. You come and see me, then you and I together go to bank to pay what you need to pay.

F: I have to make the payment for the clearance here before they could sign the document of the contract.

Now you make me feel am looking for a way to extra or export money from you I feel so bad and sad.

If you don't want to help me let me know because I feel sad and ashamed for asking you for assistance.

3G: No. I have to see you first.

F: I need to make the payment before I can come and meet you, and if you can't help me with it, It's better we forget about it because I don't really like stress I wish you're in my shoe are you going to feel better if am telling you this. Please am frustrated right now and you really want to stress again and you doubt me too.

3G: I hope you are real, but need to be proved.

F: Don't ever doubt me and if you really love me.

3G: Love is one thing, you can check me also.

F: I love you and I want to be with you forever together.

If you don't believe me it's better we stop texting each other, I pray my help will come, I wish I have the money I need I will never ask you for money.

3G: Thank you very much. I have to see you, you come to my city, you and I together go to bank to pay.

If you were me, what you would do?

F: If you can't trust me maybe you can keep your money because I don't like stress.

If you want to assist me, do it with your mind and if you're in my shoes I would help you without asking you to explain.

3G: You can do whatever you like. I have to see you first. I think it is not difficult to come to my city both of us go to bank to pay it.

F: Do you want me to lose my good and my contract.

Well it's your choice and I wish you know what am going through now.

Now I know you don't love and you don't want to see me.

How am I going to leave the goods if I didn't pay the tax clearance.

3G: No. I really want to see you. Where you are now. Are you at home?

You know I have money, I want to see you first. I'll be happy to pay if seeing you.

F: Let me tell you something if I didn't pay the money before coming over to see you I would lose the contract and I will lose all what I have work for. So you want me to lose my contract because you want to see me now. Now I know you don't want me to grow in my business. You made me feel so bad and broken 😠

3G: I have prepared the everything for you already. It depends on you. I am willing to do anything for you, but I have to see you first.

F: I have to make the payment first before I can come over and if you can't help me please stop pretending that you love or want me.

Am frustrated right now, I need to get my paperwork done.

3G: It's your decision. I wish I knew your situation earlier, I could have a better idea to deal with it.

F: It's your decision if you want to help me it's up to you.

All I know is that I need to make the payment before coming over to meet you.

3G: You enjoyed movies when you called me.

Why don't you tell me before you go to Canada. You owe tax money to US, You come back to pay it. Everything should be OK.

Canada has no right to keep you there.

F: I told you the good I order, I need to pay for the tax clearance and I need to pay it.

3G: You bought it in US, You should pay it in US. I want to see you in US, then we pay it.

F: What are you trying to say you don't want to help me that's why you are doing this to me . . . If I had my account not on hold I won't even bother you at all . . . but now you want to stress me.

And it's unfair you don't have to punish me because I ask you to borrow me this and I'll pay you back the next day I get back to the state.

3G: My money is ready to use. I want to see you first. After that everything should be OK. You are my Angel, we should be proud of us we have done right.

F: If I should leave here I'll loose this project and this is my biggest project and if I should loose it I'm not sure I'll see this kind of project anymore.

This mean a lot to me and you mean a lot to me if you really love me help me out and when it's get paid I'll be in the state shortly.

3G: You are not English girl, you don't know what you talk about.

F: What do you mean by I'm not English girl?

3G: She lived in UK many years, she should know basic English.

F: I need to get by to my paperwork I'll talk to you later let me know if you change your mind and what you mean is that I shouldn't depend on you . . . I'll have to work out something to get the money and remember you promised me and promise is a debt thanks 🙏.

3G: You do what you have to do. I have to see you first.

F: Please keep your money if you want to stress me please . . . Thanks I'll look for a way to solve my problem I don't really want to stress you or stress myself.

3G: Good luck!

F: Good luck!

3G: I want to see you first. Nothing wrong with it. I knew my angel should be much more intelligent than you. Your basic English is not good at all.

F: I want to see you but you doubt me and we can never grow in this so we need to know what we want from each other.

Please I don't like stress and if you can't assist it's better I need to get this done myself without distraction.

You promise and failed. How I wish I can do this without asking for assistance in the first place you won't even be telling me this.

Well Good luck on your search for another woman God bless you

3G: My angel had a good education. She is nice. I don't know who you are. If you are my angel, you should tell this story earlier. I'm willing to help, I want to see you first.

F: Your angel is the one texting you.

3G: I wish.

F: And you don't want to assist me keep your money because I know my God will send a(n) helper to me I believe that and you will be ashamed

3G: OK. Good luck.

F: Good luck 👍

What made you decide not to help me because this unlike you.

I feel heartbroken 💔 and sad.

Wednesday, July 14, 2021

F: You left me because you feel unsecured.
You're calling me now.
3G: No.
F: Am busy and besides you thinking I will collect your money and never contact again.
Am a woman of my word!

Are you there?

Hello!
You stopped texting me because you don't want to help me.

Wednesday July 14, 2021

I wrote an email to Fantasy.

Dear Fantasy:
I really don't know who you are? You are totally different from who in the message conversation. Why?
You know I am writer who can make and write stories. The story we have in email looks real. After that totally changed. This is unfair to me.
Anyway, it's over. I hope you well and happy. Don't do this again.
Thank you very much.
I enjoyed the person who wrote emails to me. I realized who did message is not you.

Thanks God, I am not smart enough. Finally I found out you are different from who texted message to me. 3G

Thursday, July 15, 2021

Fantasy texted a message to me:

> My greatest wish is to spend the whole day cuddling in bed with you. Good morning my king.
> 6:35 AM

Saturday, July 17, 2021

F: Hello
End.

CHAPTER FIVE
Key Points of the Possible Fraudulence

What made me concerned is the following:

1. She refused to let me see her first, then make a payment as requested.

2. Through texting messages it clearly shows that she is able to pay the government tax clearance as requested, because she said she doesn't trade stock as I do, but she invests on Bitcoin. At that time, one Bitcoin was worth about $45,000. She owed the government the tax clearance money, which was a little less than one Bitcoin in the market value. If she sold one Bitcoin in the stock market, she could pay what she owed to Tax clearance as requested.

3. Her project was worth 9 million to 18 million USD. She only spent about 3 weeks and gave one presentation, after that the committee approved the contract for her. It's too good to be true.

4. Remember the picture she sent to me after she got Canada by the PRIVATE JET, looks so beautiful, but the jet is not in working status in my mind, because the seats are not bolted to the jet floor as they should be.

5. During the texting conversation, I asked her whether she needed money to book an airline ticket. She indirectly answered that she can schedule a "flight to the nearest airport around you." If so, she should not have any problems paying Tax clearance. From this point on, in my concerns she didn't tell me the true story. I even doubt she went to Canada. She just said it to make her story more amazing and fantastic. That's all.

6. When I asked her the account # to pay the money, she hesitated to give it to me. She said she wouldn't get it until I am ready to pay.

7. She was just interested in getting money, did not show any interest in what I do, such as writing books.

Etc.

Of course, all of this is just speculation. That's why I had to see her first before paying any money as she required. Actually I had really prepared the exact amount of money that she needed.

Unfortunately, that is the only way I could do things, in order to protect myself.

Thank you guys for spending some time to read the story I wrote. Hopefully you guys can learn something special from my unbelievable online dating story.

Good luck!!!

www.ingramcontent.com/pod-product-compliance
Lightning Source LLC
LaVergne TN
LVHW041543060526
838200LV00037B/1123